THE ART
OF DANCING

THE ART
OF DANCING

A POEM IN THREE CANTOS

BY

SOAME JENYNS

1729 EDITION

EDITED
AND WITH AN INTRODUCTION
BY
ANNE COTTIS

DANCE BOOKS LTD

9 CECIL COURT LONDON WC2

First published in this edition 1978
by Dance Books Ltd
9 Cecil Court London WC2N 4EZ
Printed in Great Britain by
W & J Mackay Limited, Chatham
All rights reserved

ISBN 0 903 102 35 8 (cloth)
ISBN 0 903 102 36 6 (paper)

© 1978 Dance Books Ltd

Introduction

SOAME JENYNS lived between 1704 and 1787. In 1722 he entered St. John's College, Cambridge, and left in 1725 without a degree. Between 1742 and 1780 he was a member of parliament, mainly representing either the county or the borough of Cambridge. The copyright of his published works was left to Charles Nalson Cole who, according to instructions, saw that they were published collectively after Soame Jenyns' death. The complete works consist of both poetry and prose, and cover a field of interest ranging from the religious and moral to the metaphysical and political.

The Art of Dancing, the first of his poems to be published, appeared anonymously. I have been unable to confirm comments that it was "published in 1727" or "written in the year 1728", and the text on which this edition is based is from a copy in the British Library dated 1729. In 1748 the poem appears in a collection of contemporary works, and this second edition, dedicated to Lady Fanny Fielding—distinguished both for her beauty and her dancing—is the version which continued to be published both during and after Soame Jenyns' lifetime.

The original version was published as a poem in three cantos, as the following text shows, but the subsequent edi-

[7]

tion was re-organised by Soame Jenyns into two cantos and reduced in length. This was achieved both by removing whole areas and significantly reducing others. The following areas were removed: an invocation of several deities concerned in this art, and the rise and progress of dancing—from canto I; the description of a masquerade, and of rope dancing—from canto II; old folks cause much mischief in balls, illustrated by the example of Herodia dancing before Herod—from canto III. The sections which were significantly reduced are: the story of the institution of the star and garter by King Edward III from Canto I; and an encomium upon the genius of the nation from canto II. Throughout the second version of the poem short sections have been condensed; for example, the four lines describing the milkmaid in the first canto were reduced to the following two lines:

> The milk-maid safe thro' driving rains and snows,
> Wrapt in her cloak, and prop'd on pattens goes.

Technically this gives the poem greater control, but the rambling style and greater range of material in the first edition is something which is worth preserving.

The poem is an excellent introduction to the kind of dancing which was practised in the mid-eighteenth century. Soame Jenyns was right in his praise of Feuillet's "lasting volumes". Isaac's rigadoon was first published in 1706 and a copy has been preserved in the British Library. It is a light, quick, gay dance full of jumps and hops, and was notated in the Beauchamp/Feuillet system. The Britagne, mentioned in the second canto, may also refer to another dance composed by Isaac appearing in the same collection; there is a dance entitled the Brittania which contains a composed minuet. Examples of all the other dance forms mentioned—borees,

[8]

louvres, courants and jiggs—can be found in the collections of dances which have been republished in facsimile editions, and John Weaver's translation of Feuillet's *Chorégraphie* provides the key to the notation system.

The number of occasions when the minuet is mentioned in the poem indicate its popularity, and later in the century it replaced the other "French" dances which opened the Ball. In the second edition the following six lines appear:

> Now when the minuet oft repeated o'er,
> (Like all terrestrial joys) can please no more,
> And every nymph, refusing to expand
> Her charms, declines the circulating hand;
> Then let the jovial country-dance begin,
> And the loud fiddles call each straggler in.

These, in fact, are the only six lines which cannot be traced in the first edition of the poem.

These more formal dances were very precise in their manner of performance and required a great deal of control to dance in the way in which they are described in the first two lines of the poem. The constant change of steps in Isaac's rigadoon requires an excellent memory. The minuet probably gained in popularity because, although its basic step is precise, it became acceptable to dance it using this basic step alone. The passing and re-passing of the partners using a figure Z as a floor pattern, and the presenting of one or both hands as the partners circled around each other, are the distinguishing features of the minuet. Several dancing masters declared it to be the basis of all good dancing. Cyril Beaumont's translation of Rameau's *Le Maitre à Danser* and Kellom Tomlinson's *The Art of Dancing* contain much general information as well as verbal descriptions of the steps and manner of perform-

[9]

ance of the minuet, and other contemporary dance steps.

English country dances were printed by John Playford and his successors between 1651 and 1728, and in these the figures of the dance are described verbally and related to the phrases of the music. Feuillet devised a simplified version of his notation system so that a series of diagrams described the figures of the dances, as well as relating them to the phrases of the music. Soame Jenyns refers to the greater freedom of the steps, and John Essex, in his book *For the Further Improvement of Dancing*, published in 1710, states that "little skips are more in fashion".

In this edition of the poem spelling, use of capital letters, and italicised words and phrases have been brought more into line with twentieth century usage.

ANNE COTTIS

Anne Cottis is the Head of the Dance Department at Rolle College, Exmouth; and has been a member of the Dolmetsch Historical Dance Society since its inauguration in 1970. She has had several articles published in the Society's annual journal, has taught and lectured at its summer school for the last four years as well as teaching on its courses, and is an active committee member.

The College and the Society have actively encouraged her research into the historical area, which is only a small part of her interest in the field of dance. This was originally initiated by her study of the subject at Lady Mabel College.

During the academic year 1976–1977 she was granted a year's study leave from Rolle College to pursue her research into dance in England from 1650 to 1750.

CANTO I
The Argument

The proposition. An invocation of several deities concerned in this art. The rise and progress of dancing. An encomium upon the ancients, who admired this art. Habits proper for men in dancing, with several useful rules and cautions. Habits proper for the ladies, with a caution against painting; as also against hoops, lappetts, ruffles, fringes, etc. A memorandum to the fair, to tie their garters fast, which introduces the story of the institution of the star and garter by King Edward III. The description and praise of the fan, with an episode on the invention of that instrument; which concludes this canto.

In the smooth dance to move with graceful mien,
Easy, with care, and sprightly, tho' serene;
To mark th'instructions echoing strains convey,
And with just steps each tuneful note obey;
With nicest art to tread the circling round;
Where use the lowly sink, or nimble bound,
I sing.—Be present all ye sacred choir,
Blow the soft flute, and strike the sounding lyre.
When Fielding bids, your kind assistance bring,
And at her feet the humble tribute fling:
Oh! may her eyes (to her this verse is due)
What first themselves inspired, vouchsafe to view!

And you, celestial Venus, power divine!
Around whose throne, and ever-sacred shrine,
Unnumbered loves, and smiles, and graces fly,
Fanning with painted wings the crystal sky;
If ever you with pleasure have surveyed
The sacred dance beneath the Cretan shade,
Hither with all your little sportive throng
Descend, fair Queen, and aid your poet's song.

Nor thou, that rul'st the spacious heav'ns above,
Disdain this humble theme, almighty Jove!
For thee this art from prudent Rhea 'rose,
Invented first to cheat thy savage foes;
For thee she bade th'instructed tribe advance,
And lead thro' various rings the mystic dance.
For thee she bade shrill trumpets shake the skies,
(Ingenious thought!) to drown thy infant cries;
Whilst thy pale nurse, all trembling and afraid,
Safe thro' the crowd her heav'nly charge conveyed.

Hence to mankind the heav'n-born science flew,
And one great part of their religion grew:
The gracious powers above, they wisely thought,
Must sure approve what first themselves had taught:
Then did the priests, on each great solemn day,
(Nor yet too lazy for to dance or pray)
With mystic steps and sprightly bounds advance,
And round the sweet-perfuming altars dance:
Whilst the wide fanes, and vaulted roofs around
With swelling notes and echoing strains resound.
Pleased with the holy pomp, all heav'n attends,
And winged with music every prayer ascends.

Hail happier age! hail illustrious days!
Then arts received their just rewards of praise.
Then music, sculpture, painting did abound,
And fame and profit every artist crowned.
Then laurel's wreaths adorned the victor's head,
Whilst humbler bays poetic brows o'erspread.
Nor did the dancer's generous science claim
Inferior gains, or a less share of fame:

To him the great did all their stores disclose;
To him erected marble statues rose:
Heroes and Kings the pleasing art approved,
And gloried to excel in what they loved.
To curb the steed, and hurl the pointed dart,
Was then esteemed but half the warrior's part;
Each perfect hero equally was skilled
To grace the Ball, and glitter in the field:
Not all his triumphs gained, and battles won,
Nations subdued, and flaming towns o'erthrown,
E'er purchased Pyrrhus half that share of fame,
As that one dance, that yets records his name.

Nor did philosophers, more learned than wise,
In those bless'd times this useful art despise:
They taught, the pleasing exercise was good
To clear the brain, and purify the Blood,
To make the languid spirits briskly flow,
And ruddy cheeks with healthful blushes glow.
Th'Athenian sage, for learning ever known,
Whom sacred Phoebus from the Delphic throne
The wisest of mankind did once declare,
Thought not the dance unworthy of his care,
Ev'n when old-age and withering years had shed
Their hoary honours on his snowy head,
The wise philosopher this art pursued
To string his nerves, and warm his freezing blood.

Then poetry was too the dancer's friend,
And all the muses did his steps attend:
With equal grace, in Hesiod's sacred lines,
Ev'n yet the hero and the dancer shines:

"Valour to some, he says, the Gods impart;
To some a genius for the dancing art."
Ev'n yet, in Homer's lofty verse, is seen
Merion's engaging step, and graceful mien:
Still in the dance he charms our wond'ring eyes,
And Greeks and Trojans yield to him the prize.

But stop, my roving muse, no farther stray,
But hasten to pursue thy destined way:
Say first what dresses most the Ball adorn,
And in the active dance are easiest worn.

The rosy milk-maid, that each morning treads
On the soft carpet of the dewy meads,
With petticoats tucked up on pattens goes,
And scorns the summer's showers, or wint'ry snows;
While the proud city dames, luxuriant fair!
That ever loll within a velvet chair,
Still have their feet that fear to touch the ground
In richest silks and shining silver bound.
The soldiers nodding plumes, and scarlet red,
Shew that his life in blood and slaughter's led:
Whilst the lawn band, beneath a double chin,
As plainly speaks divinity within:
Thus each man's habit with his business suits;
Nor must we ride in pumps, or dance in boots.

But you, that oft in circling dances wheel,
Thin be your yielding sole, and low your heel:
Let no unwieldy pride your shoulders press,
But airy, light, and easy be your dress;
Let not the sword, in silken bondage tied,
An useless weight, hang lugging at your side;

No such rough weapons here will gain the prize,
No wounds we fear, but from the fair-one's eyes.
The woolly drab, and English broad-cloth warm,
Guard well the horseman from the beating storm,
But load the dancer with too great a weight,
And call from every pore a dewy sweat;
Rather let him his active limbs display
In camblet thin and glossy paduasoy.

But let not vulgar rules delay my song,
Nor precepts known to all my verse prolong:
Why should I now the gallant spark command
With clean white gloves to fit his ready hand;
Or in his fob enlivening spirits wear,
And quick'ning salts, to raise the fainting fair?
Why should my lays the youthful tribe advise,
Lest snowy clouds from out their wigs arise?
So shall their partners mourn their laces spoiled,
And shining silks with greasy powder soiled.
Nor need I sure bid prudent youths beware
Lest with erected tongues their buckles stare;
The pointed steel shall oft their stockings rend,
And oft the approaching petticoat offend.

And now, ye youthful fair, I sing to you;
With pleasing smiles my useful labours view;
For you the silkworms fine-wrought webs display,
And lab'ring spin their little lives away:
For you bright gems with radiant colours glow,
Fair as the dyes that paint the heavenly bow:
For you the sea resigns its pearly store,
And earth unlocks her mines of treasured ore;

[17]

In vain yet nature thus her gifts bestows,
Unless those gifts your selves with art dispose.

But think not, nymphs, that in the glittering Ball
One form of dress prescribed can suit with all:
One brightest shines when wealth and art combine
To make the lovely piece completely fine.
In dishabille another steals our hearts,
And, rich in native beauties, wants not art's.
In some are such resistless beauties found,
That in all dresses they are sure to wound:
Their heav'nly forms all foreign aids despise,
And gems but borrow lustre from their eyes.
Such oft, Brittania, in thy court appear,
Famed ev'n in beauty's seat, where all are fair,
And blaze like planets in a starry night,
'Midst vulgar beauties, with distinguished light.
So Queensburgh, Manchester, and Bedford shine;
Such charms are Cootes, such lovely Fielding thine.

Let the fair nymph, in whose plump cheeks is seen
A constant blush, be clad in verdant green;
In such a dress the sporting sea-nymphs go;
So in their grassy beds fresh roses blow:
The lass whose skin is like the hazel brown,
With brighter yellow should o'ercome her own,
But the fair maid, in whose pale cheeks of snow
No blushes rise, nor blooming roses glow,
Far above all should potent scarlet fly,
And soonest choose the sable's mournful dye:
So the pale moon still shines with purest light
Clothed in the dusky mantle of the night.

[18]

But far from you be all those treach'rous arts,
That wound with painted charms unwary hearts.
Dancing's a touchstone that true beauty tries,
Nor suffers charms that natures hand denies.
Tho' for a while we may with wonder view
The rosy blush, and skin of lovely hue,
Yet soon the dance will cause the cheeks to glow,
And melt the coral lips, and neck of snow.

So shine the fields in icy fetters bound,
Whilst frozen gems bespangle all the ground:
Thro' the clear crystal of the glitt'ring snow,
With scarlet red the blushing hawthorns glow;
O'er all the plain unnumbered glories rise,
And a new bright creation charms the eyes;
Till spring at length, with Zephyr's gentle winds
And warming gales, the frozen glebe unbinds;
Then straight at once the glitt'ring scenes decay,
And all the transient glories fade away;
The fields resign the beauties not their own,
And all their snowy charms run trickling down.

Dare I in such momentous points advise,
I should condemn the hoop's enormous size:
Oft hath myself the inconvenience found;
Oft have I trod th'immeasurable round,
And mourned my shins bruised black with many a wound.
Nor should the tightened stays, too straightly laced,
In whalebone bondage gall the slender waist;
Nor waving lappets should the dancing fair
Nor ruffles edged with dangling fringes wear:
Oft will the cobweb ornaments catch hold

[19]

On the approaching button rough with gold;
Nor force, nor art can then the bonds divide
When once th'entangled Gordian knot is tied:
So th'unhappy pair, by Hymen's Power,
Together joined in some ill-fated hour,
The more they strive their freedom to regain,
The faster binds th'indissoluble chain.

Let each fair nymph that fears to be disgraced,
Ever be sure to tie her garters fast,
Lest the loosed string, amidst the public Ball,
A wished-for prize to some proud fop should fall,
Who the rich treasure shall triumphant show,
And make her cheeks with burning blushes glow.

'Tis hence the royal George and Garter blue,
Brittania's Nobles grace (if fame says true)
Once valiant Edward, of illustrious fame,
The third of England's Kings that bore the name;
With famed Plantagenet, divinely fair,
Once Britain's glory, and her monarch's care,
Led up the royal Ball with courteous air:
Loosed with the pleasing toil (as stories tell)
Down on the floor her loosened garter fell;
The gallant King catch'd up the lovely prize,
Whilst crimson blushes o'er her cheeks arise,
And bearing it aloft with joyful pride,
"Mourn not, my fair, so small a loss, he cried;
When all those blooming charms, by time decayed,
And flowing tresses shall in dust be laid;
When those all-conquering eyes, and balmy breath,
Themselves shall yield (as yield they must) to death,

[20]

This garter bright, with never-dying fame,
To endless ages shall record your name:
This mark of honour Britain's chiefs shall bear,
And sovereign Kings themselves be proud to wear."

Now let the muse my lovely charge remind,
Lest they, forgetful, leave their fans behind.
Oh! lay not, nymphs, the pretty toy aside,
A toy at once displayed for used and pride;
A wondrous engine, that by magic charms
Cools your own breasts, and ev'ry others warms!

What daring bard shall e'er attempt to tell
The pow'rs that in this little engine dwell?
What verse can e'er explain its various parts,
Its num'rous uses, motions, charms, and arts?
Its painted folds that oft, extended wide,
Th'afflicted fair-ones blubbered beauties hide;
When secret sorrows her sad bosom fill,
When Strephon is unkind, or Shock is ill:
Its sticks, on which her eyes dejected pore,
And pointing fingers numbered o'er and o'er;
When the kind virgin burns with secret shame,
Dies to consent, yet fears to own her flame;
Its shake triumphant, its victorious clap,
Its angry flutter, and its wanton tap.

Forbear, my muse, th'extensive theme to sing,
Nor trust in such a flight your tender wing;
Rather do you in humble lines proclaim
From whence this engine took its form and name:
Say from what cause it first derived its birth,
How formed in Heav'n, how thence deduced to earth.

[21]

Once in Arcadia, that famed seat of love,
There lived a nymph, the pride of all the grove,
A lovely nymph, adorned with ev'ry grace,
An easy shape, and sweetly-blooming face;
Fanny the damsel's name, as chaste as fair,
Each virgin's envy, and each swain's despair:
To charm her ear the rival shepherds sing,
Blow the soft flute, and wake the trembling string.
For her they leave their wand'ring flocks to rove,
Whilst Fanny's name resounds through ev'ry grove,
And spreads on ev'ry tree enclosed with knots of love.
As Fielding's now, her eyes all hearts enflame,
Like her in beauty, as alike in name.

'Twas when the summer sun, now mounted high,
With fiercer beams had warmed the sultry sky,
Beneath the covert of a cooling shade,
To shun the heat, this lovely nymph was laid:
The sultry weather o'er her cheeks had spread
A blush, that added to their native red:
And her fair breast, as polished marble white,
Was half concealed, and half exposed to sight.
Whilst thus she lay, the potent God passed by
Who rules the winds, and calms the troubled sky,
Aeolus, whose nod provokes the sleeping main,
And bids the raging waves be still again:
He stopped awhile, and gazed with fond delight,
And sucked in poison at the dang'rous sight:
He loved, and ventured to declare his pain,
But still he loved, and still he woo'd in vain;
The cruel nymph, regardless of his moan,
Minds not his flame; uneasy with her own,

Still she complains, that he who ruled the air
Would not command one Zephyr to repair
Around her face, nor gentle breeze to play
Thro' the dark glade, and cool the sultry day:
By love incited, and the hopes of joy,
Th'ingenious God contrived this pretty toy,
Which might, with Zephyr's, cool her glowing flame,
And callèd Fan from lovely Fanny's name.

CANTO II
The Argument.
Of French Dancing

The Assembly-room and company described. The Ball to be begun with French dances. An encomium upon the genius of the nation. The description of a Masquerade. Of the writing dances in characters, first found by Monsieur Feuillet. Each dancer ought to consult his own genius and abilities; compared to a poet. Of Stage-dancing and Rope-dancing. Several useful rules. An encomium upon this art.

Now see prepared to lead the sprightly dance
The lovely nymphs and well-dressed youths advance:
The spacious room receives its jovial guest,
And the floor shakes, with pleasing weight oppressed;
Thick ranged on every side with various dyes
The fair in shining silks our sight surprise:
So, on a grassy bed profuse of flow'rs,
With warming gales refreshed, and genial show'rs,
The lovely lillies, decked in silver snow,
And tulips that with painted beauties glow,
The blushing rose, and pinks of various hue,
The crimson hyacinth, and violet blue,
Clothed in their richest robes, together rise
And in a gay confusion charm our eyes.

   High o'er their heads, with num'rous candles bright
Large branches shed their golden beams of light;
Their golden beams, that still more brightly glow,
Reflected back from gems and eyes below.
Unnumbered fans, to cool the crowded fair,
With breathing Zephyrs move the circling air.
The sprightly fiddle, and the echoing lyre,

Each youthful breast with gen'rous warmth inspire:
Fraught with all joys, the blissful moments fly,
Whilst music melts the ear, and beauty charms the eye.

Now let the youth, to whose superior place
It first belongs the glitt'ring Ball to grace,
With humble bow and ready hand prepare
Forth from the crowd to lead his chosen fair:
The fair shall not his kind request deny,
But to the pleasing toil with equal ardour fly.

But stay, rash pair, nor yet untaught advance,
First hear the Muse e're you attempt to dance.
By art directed, o'er the foaming tide,
Secure from rocks the painted vessels glide.
By art the chariot scours the dusty plain,
Springs at the whip, and hears the strait'ning rein.
To art our bodies must obedient prove,
If e'er we hope with graceful ease to move:
Nor think, ye fair, that any native charm
Can e'er our eyes attract, or bosoms warm,
Unless you learn the rules these lines impart,
The useful precepts of the dancing Art.

First, with French-dancing be each Ball begun,
Nor Country-dance intrude till these are done:
With these the muse shall her first labours grace,
And those come after, in their proper place.

The French (if right all ancient legends tell)
In dances formed by rules did first excel:
They first this art to full perfection brought,

[28]

And certain steps by certain precepts taught:
Hence all those pleasing artful dances came
That, from their authors, we French-dances name.

Wise nature, ever with a prudent hand,
Dispenses various gifts to ev'ry land;
To ev'ry nation frugally imparts
A genius fit for some peculiar arts.
The Germans in mechanics best succeed;
The Dutch in traffick, and in war the Swede:
Brittania justly glories to have found
The farthest isles, and sailed the globe around:
Soft arts of peace adorn Italia's plains;
There painting, poetry, and music reigns;
There sweet Corelli first his viol strung;
There Raphael painted, and there Vida sung.

But Gallia all superior must confess
To ev'ry clime in dancing, and in dress:
Let great Italia boast her sons of fame,
And England shew her Drake's and Candish's name;
Germania glory to have first begun
The printing art, and formed the murd'ring gun,
France for one worthy will produce them ten,
Alike illustrious both for arts and men.
From her the sword-knot sprung, and smart toupée,
From her Legar(de) arose, and famed L'Abée.
From her, ye beaux, ye learn to charm the fair
With powdered shoulders and a janty air.
From her, ye fair, you learn a thousand arts
To conquer and secure your lovers hearts;
To frown, and smile, and lean the head aside,

Lisp, scream, and whisper, with a deal beside.
To her we all our noblest dances owe,
The sprightly Rigadoon, and Louvre slow,
The Borée, and Courant, unpractised long,
Th'immortal Minuet, and the sweet Britagne.

But most her happy genius is displayed
In forming first the splendid Masquerade;
Where all the powers of art united join
To make the Ball with perfect lustre shine:
There, as in Mahomet's well-fancied heav'n,
Rapture at once to ev'ry sense is given:
Ten thousand habits please the wand'ring sight,
With blazing gold, and glitt'ring jewels bright:
In lofty piles ambrosial sweetmeats stand,
And ripened fruits in clusters court the hand;
Nectareous wines in sparkling currents flow,
Whate'er Champaign's aspiring hills bestow,
Or on Burgundia's plains delicious grow.
Dancing the happy night with pleasure crowns,
And music thro' the vaulted roofs resounds;
Unnumbered yielding nymphs complete our joy,
For here severest prudes no more are coy;
No more they fear their careful parent's eye,
The jealous cuckold, or the watchful spy;
Here coldest maids are without blushes kind,
The mask that hides the face reveals the mind:
Or, should the tyrants strive to give us pain,
Pretend to blush, or frown, 'twere all in vain;
How should the lover fear? The kind disguise
Hides threat'ning frowns, but shews consenting eyes.

Long was the dancing art unfixed and free;
Hence lost in error and uncertainty:
No precepts did it mind, or rules obey,
But ev'ry master taught a different way:
Hence, e're each new-born dance was fully tried,
The lovely product, ev'n in blooming, died:
Tho' various hands in wild confusion tossed,
Its steps were altered, and its beauties lost:
Till Feuillet at length, great name! arose,
And did the dance in characters compose:
Each lovely grace by certain marks he taught,
And ev'ry step in lasting volumes wrote.
Hence o'er the world this pleasing art shall spread,
And ev'ry dance in ev'ry clime be read;
By distant masters shall each step be seen,
Tho' mountains rise and oceans roar between.
Hence with her sister-arts shall dancing claim
An equal right to universal fame,
And Isaac's rigadoon shall last as long
As Raphael's painting, or as Virgil's song.

Each cautious bard, e're he attempts to sing,
First gently flutt'ring, tries his tender wing,
And if he finds that with uncommon fire
A daring genius does his soul inspire,
At once to heav'n he soars in lofty odes,
And sings alone of heroes, and of Gods;
Or makes his muse in solemn tragic verse
The acts of princes, and of kings rehearse:
But if she trembling fears to soar so high,
He then descends to softer elegy;
And if despairing still he finds his wit,

For am'rous tales and elegy unfit,
Yet still he may in pastoral succeed,
And deftly tune it in an oaten reed.

So should each dancer, e're he tries to move,
With care his strength, his weight, and genius prove,
And if he finds kind nature's gifts impart
Endowments proper for the dancing art,
If in himself he feels together joined
An active body, and a sprightly mind;
In nimble rigadoons let him advance,
Or in the louvre's slow majestic dance:
But if, for want of genius, warmth, and fire,
He dares not to such noble acts aspire,
Let him, contented with an easy pace,
The gentle minuet's circling mazes trace;
If this too hard shall seem, let him forbear,
And to the Country-dance confine his care.

True dancing, like true wit, is best expressed
By nature, only to advantage dressed:
'Tis not a nimble bound, or caper high,
That can pretend to please a curious eye;
Good judges no such tumblers tricks regard,
Or think them beautiful because they're hard:
Yet in Stage-dancing, if performed with skill,
Such active feats our eyes with wonder fill;
And some there are, that of uncommon frame
Have thro' these arduous paths sought out for fame:
That Pindar Rich despises vulgar roads,
And soars an eagle's height above the clouds,
Whilst humbler dancers, fearful how they climb,

But buzz below amidst the flow'ry thyme:
Now soft and slow he bends the circling round,
Now rises high upon the sprightly bound,
Now springs aloft, too swift for mortal sight,
Now falls unhurt from some stupendous height;
Like Proteus, in a thousand forms is seen,
Sometimes a god, sometimes an harlequin.

Nor here, my muse, must we forget to name
Those bold advent'rers on the rope for fame,
See how the nimble youth, now mounted high,
Appears without the aid of wings to fly!
Like Maia's son, the messenger of Jove,
He seems to bring some orders from above;
And unconcerned looks down on crowds below,
That gaze, and tremble, but to see him go.
So thousands on the shore admiring stood,
When Daedalus flew o'er the Cretan flood.

What will not man attempt when led by fame?
What toils or dangers can ambition tame?
In vain has prudent nature's wise commands
With foaming seas divided distant lands;
Proud o'er th'inviolable bounds to leap,
With sails and oars they travel o'er the deep:
In vain high-tow'ring pinions she denies,
Art by a slender cord the want supplies;
Secure on this the nimble artist swings,
Nor fears the sun should melt his waxen wings.

In vain we learn to trace a certain round,
And know exactly where to sink and bound;

[33]

In ev'ry movement there must still be seen
A nameless grace, and a becoming mien:
In vain a Master shall employ his care
Where nature once has fixed a clumsy air;
Rather let such, to country sports confined,
Pursue the flying hare, and tim'rous hind:
To chase his fellow-beasts be still his game,
And rural conquests his sublimest fame,
But ne'er to these politer arts aspire,
Or hope to soar above a country squire.

Nor yet, while I an awkward clown despise,
Would I a soft effem'nate air advise;
With equal scorn I would the fop deride,
Nor let him dance, but on the woman's side.

And you, fair nymphs, avoid with equal care,
A stupid dullness, and a coquet air;
Neither with eyes that ever love the ground,
Asleep, like spinning tops, run round and round;
Nor yet with giddy looks, and wanton pride,
Stare all around, and skip from side to side.

Would you in dancing ev'ry fault avoid,
To keep true time be your first thoughts employed;
All other errors they in vain shall mend
Who in this one important point offend.
For this, when now united hand in hand,
Eager to start the youthful couple stand,
Let them awhile their nimble feet restrain,
And with soft taps beat time to ev'ry strain:
So two sleek racers on Newmarket plains,
Whom scarce the bit can hold, or streight'ning reins,

[34]

Impatient o'er the velvet turf to bound,
With trampling feet spurn up the verdant ground.

　'Tis not enough that ev'ry stander-by
No glaring errors on your steps can spy;
The dance and music must so nicely meet,
Each note must seem an echo to your feet:
A nameless grace must on each movement dwell,
Which words can ne'er express, nor precepts tell;
Not to be taught, but ever to be seen
In sweet Camarthen's air, and Gore's engaging mien:
'Tis such an air that makes her thousands fall
When Fielding dances at a birth-night Ball;
Smooth as Camilla she skims o'er the plain,
And flies, like her, thro' crowds of heroes slain.

　Hail loveliest Art! that canst all hearts ensnare,
And make the fairest still appear more fair!
Beauty can little execution do
Unless she borrows half her arms from you:
Few like Pygmalion doat on lifeless charms,
Or care to clasp a statue in their arms;
But breasts of flint must melt with soft desire
When art and motion wake the sleeping fire.
A Venus drawn by great Apelles's hand
May for a while our wond'ring eyes command,
But still, tho' formed with all the pow'rs of art,
The lifeless piece can never warm the heart:
So a fair nymph, perhaps, may please the eye,
Whilst all her beauteous limbs unactive lie;
But when her charms are in the dance displayed,
Then ev'ry heart adores the lovely maid:

[35]

This sets her beauty in the fairest light,
And shews each grace in full perfection bright;
Then, as she turns around, from ev'ry part,
Like porcupines, she send a piercing dart:
In vain, alas! the fond spectator tries
To shun the pleasing dangers of her eyes,
For, Parthian like, she wounds as sure behind
With lovely curls, and ivory neck reclined;
Whether her steps the minuet's mazes trace,
Or the slow louvre's more majestic pace;
Whether the rigadoon employs her care,
Or sprightly jigg displays the nimble fair;
At ev'ry step new beauties we explore,
And worship now what we admired before.

So when Aeneas in the Tyrian grove
Fair Venus met, the charming Queen of love,
The beauteous goddess, whilst unmov'd she stood,
Seemed some fair nymph, the guardian of the wood;
But when she moved, at once her heav'nly mien
And graceful step confess bright beauty's Queen;
New glories o'er her form each moment rise,
And all the goddess opens to his eyes.

CANTO III

The Argument.
Of Country-Dancing

The rise and progress of Country-dancing: compared to the Theatre. Rules to be observed on choosing our partners. Old folks cause much mischief in Balls; illustrated by the example of Herodia dancing before Herod. The Country–dance described. Useful morals to be learned from several Country–dances. Several rules to be observed in and after dancing. The conclusion of the whole.

When good King Arthur, in the days of yore,
The British crown and royal sceptre bore,
In some fair op'ning glade, each summer's night,
Where Cynthia shed her silver beams of light,
The jocund fairies sprightly dances led
On the soft carpet of a grassy bed;
Some, with the pigmy king, and little queen,
In circling ringlets marked the level green:
Some bade soft flutes and mellow pipes resound,
And music warble thro' the groves around.

   Oft lonely shepherds, as they piping sate,
Oft from their daily toil returning late,
Belated peasants, by the forest's side,
Their wanton sports and merry revels 'spy'd.
Instructed hence, throughout the British Isle,
And fond to imitate the pleasing toil,
The nut-brown maids and nimble swains resort
To ev'ry wake to try the pretty sport.
Oft as returns the merry month of May,
When the green plains their richest robes display
'Round, where the trembling pole is fixed on high,

And bears its flow'ry honours to the sky:
The youthful couples nimble dances lead,
And rural belles the verdant fields o'erspread.
Here Bumkinet, arrayed in doublet new,
With ruddy Marian, fine with ribbons blue;
There Blousilinda, decked in pinners clean,
With gentle Colin treads the level green:
On ev'ry side Aeolian artists stand,
Whose lab'ring elbows swelling winds command:
The swelling winds harmonious pipes inspire,
And wake in ev'ry breast a gen'rous fire.

Thus taught at first the Country-dance began
And hence to cities and to courts it ran:
Succeeding ages did in time impart
Various improvements to the Noble Art:
From fields and groves to palaces removed,
Great ones the pleasing exercise approved:
Hence sprightly fiddles and shrill trumpets sound,
And echo thro' the vaulted roofs around:
Bright gems and silks, brocades and ribbons join
To make the Ball with perfect glory shine.

So rude at first the tragic muse appeared,
Her voice alone by rustic rabble heard,
Where twisting trees a cooling arbour made,
The pleased spectators sate beneath a shade:
The homely stage with rushes green was strowed,
And in a cart the strolling actors rode:
Till time at length improved the great design,
And bade the scenes with painted landskips shine:
Then art did all the bright machines dispose,

And theatres of Parian marble rose:
Then mimic thunder shook the trembling sky,
Ands Gods descended from their tow'rs on high.

  With caution now let ev'ry youth prepare
To choose a partner from the mingled fair:
Vain would be here th'instructing muse's voice
If she pretended to direct his choice,
Beauty by fancy is alone expressed,
And charms in diff'rent forms each diff'rent breast:
A snowy skin this am'rous youth admires,
Whilst nut-brown cheeks another's bosom fires.
Small waists and slender limbs some hearts ensnare,
Whilst others love the more substantial fair.

  But let not outward charms your judgements sway,
Your reason rather than your eyes obey;
And in the dance, as in the marriage noose,
Rather for merit than for beauty choose:
Be her your choice who knows with perfect skill
When she should move, and when she should be still;
That uninstructed can perform her share,
And kindly half the pleasing burthen bear.
Unhappy is that hopeless wretch's fate
Who, fetter'd in the matrimonial state,
With a poor, simple unexperienced wife
Is forced to lead the tedious dance of life:
And such is his with such a partner joined;
A moving puppet, but without a mind:
Still must his hand be pointing out the way,
Yet ne'er can teach so fast as she can stray;
Beneath her follies he must ever groan,
And ever blush for errors not his own.

[41]

But now behold! united hand in hand,
Ranged on each side the well-paired couples stand:
With secret joy, and with a fond delight,
Each gen'rous youth expects the pleasing fight;
Whilst lovely eyes, that flash unusual rays,
And snowy bubbies pulled above the stays;
Whilst busy hands and bridling heads declare
The eager nymphs, and the impatient fair;
Far hence removed be ev'ry stander-by
That views our pleasures with a cens'ring eye:
Far hence be all on whose severer brow
Old-age has left the furrows of his plough;
Those surly critics ever mirth destroy,
And spoil all pleasures which they can't enjoy.
Let no discreet mamma call miss aside,
And her unguarded pretty freedoms chide,
With angry frowns compel her to be coy,
And all her partner's pleasing hopes destroy;
'Tis such that fill each harmless virgin's brain
With affectation, and with cold disdain,
And strive their native innocence to hide
With all their sex's artifice and pride;
That gravely preach to the good-natured fair,
A squeeze is more than virtue ought to bear;
A kiss so much a lady's honour stains,
Marriage, or death alone, her fame regains:
And of Lucretia talk, that foolish prude,
Who stabbed herself because her spark was rude:
'Tis from such notions that old folks instill
That frequent quarrels our Assemblies fill,
And Balls, designed for mirth, too oft conclude
By sad mishap in marriage, or in blood.

[42]

Thus, when Herodia (that fair fatal name.
At once the dancers glory, and their shame)
In the smooth dance her beauteous form displayed,
All Herod's court admired the lovely maid:
A thousand hearts her beauteous form adored,
But Herod's most, Judea's tyrant-lord:
With joy he viewed her trace the winding round,
And felt at ev'ry step a pleasing wound.
Now on her flowing hair he fixed his eyes;
Now on her breasts, that gently fall and rise;
Now views her cheeks, with pure vermillion red,
And balmy lips, with blooming roses spread:
Where-e'er she moved, his heart and eyes pursued,
Till love, the greater tyrant, had the less subdued.
Scarce had she done, when to the lovely maid,
Grasping her hand, the royal captive said,
"By heav'n, and all its gracious powers, I swear,
May heaven th'irrevocable promise hear;
By those all-conquering eyes, and this fair hand,
Which can the hearts of captive kings command,
If in the power of Herod's awful throne,
Name but your wish, and 'tis already done."
Her watchful mother heard the sacred vow,
Whilst fierce revenge sate heavy on her brow;
(For long had John's reforming voice decried
Her impious life, her incest, and her pride,)
Close to her side she called the lovely maid,
And forced her to demand the Baptist's head.
The lovely maid with tears and sighs complied,
And for her wish the holy martyr died:
Oh, cruel mother! too obedient fair!
How could you thus a tender heart ensnare?

You, pretty miss, had not her counsels swayed,
For a fine watch, or sparkling ring, had prayed;
A gilded chariot you perhaps had chose,
A diamond necklace, or a suit of clothes;
Or had you your most fav'rite wish pursued,
For a fine monkey, or a husband sued;
But sure your tender heart, unused to ill,
Could ne'er have plotted sacred blood to spill,
Had not your tongue mamma's commands obeyed,
Led by her counsels, of her threats afraid.

With mortal breasts revenge and malice fill,
What won't they render instruments of ill?
Religion long has been profanely made
By hypocrites and priests a gainful trade;
And Law, which by its founders was designed
To be the careful guardian of mankind,
Is, long since, grown but a pretence to cheat,
T'oppress the poor, and shield th'oppressing great.
Thus dancing too, we find, was forced to be
Bawd to a woman's lust and cruelty.

But see! the sprightly dance is now begun;
Now here, now there the giddy maze they run:
Now with swift steps they pace the circling ring;
Now all confused too swift for sight they spring:
So, in a wheel with rapid fury tossed,
The undistinguished spokes are in the motion lost.

The dancer here no more requires a guide,
To no strict steps his nimble feet are tied:
The muse's precepts here would useless be,

[44]

Where all is fancied, unconfined, and free:
Let him but to the music's voice attend,
By this instructed, he can ne'er offend.
If to his share it falls the dance to lead,
In well-known paths he may be sure to tread;
If others lead, let him their motions view,
And in their steps the winding maze pursue.

A thoughtful head, and a reflecting mind,
Can in each dance an useful moral find:
In Hunt-the-Squirrel thus, the nymph we view,
Seeks when we fly, but flies when we pursue:
Thus in round-dances, where our partners change,
And unconfined from fair to fair we range:
As soon as one from his own consort flies,
Another seizes on the lovely prize;
A while the fav'rite youth enjoys her charms,
Till the next-comer steals her from his arms;
The former then no more is worth her care:
How true an emblem of th'inconstant fair!

Where can philosophers and sages wise,
That read the curious volumes of the skies,
A model more exact than dancing name
Of the creations universal frame?
Where worlds unnumbered o'er th'aetherial way
In a bright regular confusion stray:
Now here, now there they whirl along the sky,
Now near approach, and now far distant fly;
Now meet in the same order they begun,
And then the great celestial dance is done.

Where can the moralist find a juster plan
Of the vain errors and the life of man?
A while thro' justling crowds we toil and sweat,
And eagerly pursue we know not what;
Then, when our little trifling race is run,
Quite tired, sit down just were we first begun.

Tho' to your arms kind fate's indulgent care
Has giv'n a partner exquisitely fair,
Let not her charms so much engage your heart
That you neglect the skilful dancer's part:
Be not, when you the tuneful notes should hear
Still whis'pring idle prattle in her ear:
Whilst you should be employed, be not at play,
Nor for your joys all other steps delay;
But when the finished dance you once have done,
And with applause thro' ev'ry couple run,
There rest awhile: – There snatch the fleeting bliss,
The tender whisper, and the balmy kiss;
Each secret wish, each softer hope confess,
And with your hand her panting bubbies press;
With smiles the fair shall hear your warm desires,
While music softens, and while dancing fires.

Thus, mixed with love, the pleasing toil pursue
Till the unwelcome morn appears to view,
Then when approaching day its beams displays,
And the dull candles shine with fainter rays;
Then when the sun just rises o'er the deep,
And each bright eye is almost set in sleep,
With ready hands, obsequious youths, prepare
Safe to their homes to lead each chosen fair,

[46]

And guard her from the morn's inclement air.
Let a warm hood enwrap her lovely head,
And o'er her neck a handkerchief be spread;
Around her shoulders let this arm be cast,
While that defends from cold her slender waist;
With kisses warm her balmy lips shall glow,
Unchilled by nightly damps, or wint'ry snow;
Whilst gen'rous white wine, mulled with ginger warm,
Shall safely guard her inward frame from harm.

But ever let my lovely pupils fear
To chill their mantling blood with cold small-beer:
Ah, thoughtless fair! the tempting draught refuse,
When thus forewarned by my experienced muse.
Let the ill consequence your thoughts employ,
Nor hazard future pains for present joy;
Destruction lurks within the pois'nous dose,
A fatal fever, or a pimpled nose.

Thus thro' each precept of the dancing art
The muse has played the kind instructors part;
Thro' ev'ry maze her pupils she has led,
And pointed out the surest paths to tread;
No more remains, no more the goddess sings,
But drops her pinions, and unfurls her wings;
On downy beds the wearied dancers lie,
And sleep's silk cords tie down each drowsy eye,
Delightful dreams their pleasing sports restore,
And, ev'n in sleep, they seem to dance once more.

And now complete my gen'rous labours lie,
Which shall the pow'r of death and time defy,

[47]

So long as birds shall cleave the yielding air,
And gallant youths to glitt'ring Balls repair;
So long as fish in silver streams we find,
And damsels fret with aged partners joined;
So long as nymphs shall, with attentive ear,
A fiddle, rather than a sermon, hear;
So long the brightest eyes shall oft peruse
These useful lines of my instructive muse:
Each belle shall wear them wrote upon her fan,
And each bright beau shall read 'em – if he can.

FINIS